Another Kind of Hero:
Preparing Successors for Leadership

Craig E. Aronoff, Ph.D. and
John L. Ward, Ph.D.

Family Business Leadership Series, No. 3

Family Enterprise Publishers
P.O. Box 4356
Marietta, GA 30061-4356

ISSN: 1071-5010
ISBN: 0-9651011-3-4
© 1992
Fifth Printing

Family Business Leadership Series

We believe that family businesses are special, not only to the families that own and manage them but to our society and to the private enterprise system. Having worked and interacted with hundreds of family enterprises in the past twenty years, we offer the insights of that experience and the collected wisdom of the world's best and most successful family firms.

This volume is a part of a series offering practical guidance for family businesses seeking to manage the special challenges and opportunities confronting them.

To order additional copies, contact:
    Family Enterprise Publishers
    1220-B Kennestone Circle
    Marietta, Georgia 30066
    Tel: 1-800-551-0633
    Web Site: www.efamilybusiness.com

Quantity discounts are available.

Other volumes in the series include:

Family Business Succession: The Final Test of Greatness

Family Meetings: How to Build a Stronger Family and a Stronger Business

How Families Work Together

Family Business Compensation

How to Choose & Use Advisors: Getting the Best Professional Family Business Advice

Financing Transitions: Managing Capital and Liquidity in the Family Business

Family Business Governance: Maximizing Family and Business Potential

Preparing Your Family Business For Strategic Change

Making Sibling Teams Work: The Next Generation

Developing Family Business Policies: Your Guide to the Future

Family Business Values: How to Assure a Legacy of Continuity and Success

More Than Family: Non-Family Executives in the Family Business

Make Change Your Family Business Tradition

Contents

Exhibits

Once upon a time there was a man who had a vision and began pursuing it. Two others saw that the first man had a vision and began following him.

In time, the children of those who followed asked their parents to describe what they saw. But what their parents described appeared to be the coattails of the man in front of them.

When the children heard this, they turned from their parents' vision, saying it was not worthy of pursuit.

— Jacob the Baker: Gentle Wisdom
for a Complicated World,
by Noah ben Shea

If the family business is to endure, its leaders must find a way to show their children more than "the coattails of the man in front of them." They must impart understanding of the founder's vision, and help their children prepare to revitalize and convey it in its full power and resonance.

Without such an effort, the current business leader's vision will begin to die with him or her.

The Importance of Successor Development

In most family businesses today, developing future leaders takes low priority.

Nurturing new leadership does not come naturally to most entrepreneurs. Even if they hope for continuity, most business owners don't adequately address their children's preparation for leadership.

Instead, many take the "Let's give Jimmy a try" approach, tossing a successor candidate into a tough job with no preparation. Other families wait until the business owner is incapacitated — or dead — before letting the next generation plunge in. Another route is to have the successor plod through the organization, filling whatever jobs that open up. Others take the "silver spoon approach," sheltering the successor in newly created posts such as assistant to the president that allow little real experience.

These practices seldom equip the successor for the challenges that will face family business leaders of the future.

The Road Ahead

The next generation of owner-managers will face great challenges.

The rate of change in business has accelerated so much that a single business strategy rarely endures for a generation. Consolidation in many industries has built competitors into giants with enormous financial, marketing and distribution muscle. Product lifecycles are shortening. National boundaries are crumbling. Industry definitions are disappearing. Not only must successors prepare to run the business, but they must equip themselves for strategic revitalization — not once, but perhaps many times during their tenure.

The successor must prepare for a job that doesn't yet exist, in an era no one can fully foresee. Add to this the timeless challenge of following in the footsteps of a successful and dominant business leader who may be idolized by the family and others, and the successor's job begins to look daunting indeed.

Wanted: Another Kind of Hero

In creating a business, the entrepreneur already has performed an endeavor noted writer and scholar Joseph Campbell would call "heroic" — an act by "a founder of something ... (who has) to leave the old and go in quest of the ... idea that will have the potentiality of bringing forth that new thing."

To sustain that new thing into successive generations and revitalize it, the business owner must bring forth yet another new thing: **"another kind of hero"** — a hero who, in Campbell's words, "reinterprets the tradition and makes it valid as a living experience." This booklet is about building another kind of hero — a successor who is prepared not only to follow in the current leader's footsteps, but to revitalize the family business vision by reinterpreting it for future generations.

A strong successor development program provides the best chance of maximizing the potential of the new generation of family business leadership. It can assure the company of management depth and breadth in the future. It heightens the chances of retaining talented members of the younger generation. And it can lay the groundwork for developing and retaining important nonfamily managers as the company grows.

Focus on Developmental Years

While developing family business successors is a lifelong process, this booklet focuses on the years when the 20- to 40-year-old successor candidate or candidates are working in the business in preparation for leadership. Selection of a successor

The successor must prepare for a job that doesn't yet exist, in an era no one can fully foresee.

and the transition to leadership are covered in more detail in the first booklet in **The Family Business Leadership Series**, *Family Business Succession: The Final Test of Greatness.*

This booklet does not assume that you have chosen a successor. Nor does it assume that there is only one top job for which one candidate must be prepared. Instead, it uses the word "successor" to refer to anyone who may be a candidate for a variety of top jobs on the family business management team. **Family businesses increasingly are managed by a team of successors**, and any development program should encompass career paths for candidates for all of the jobs on the team. It is also wise to plan for more than one potential successor, as discussed later.

This booklet describes seven natural stages in the growth and maturation of future business leaders. It discusses the creation of an effective personal development plan. It describes ways to cultivate successors' crucial business and leadership skills.

The booklet lays out some alternative routes up the management ladder to give successors the breadth and depth of experience they need. It offers suggestions on family relations and communications during successor development. And it details special personal challenges to both incumbent leaders and successors throughout this five- to 15-year process.

The Seven Stages in Successor Development

The making of a new generation of leaders typically encompasses seven stages.

1. **Attitude Preparation**. Important attitudes toward work and the family business are formed during a child's first 25 years of life. Usually, this stage includes part-time work in the family business and occasional business-related trips with the business owner or a mentor. Ideally, it also incorporates three-to-five years of outside work experience.

2. **Entry.** Serious, detailed discussions of succession usually shouldn't begin until the young person enters the business. This usually occurs when the successor is between 20 and 30 years of age and takes an existing, necessary job in the business. It includes training, orientation and developing relationships with other employees.

3. **Business Development.** This phase usually occurs between 25 and 35 years of age, when the successor should obtain the best job experience possible. He or she should be cultivating needed skills and abilities, including some that are complementary to those of the incumbent. On-the-job education about the business's history, culture, strategy and philosophy should occur. If a successor isn't the best

candidate for leadership, it will usually become obvious during this stage.

4. **Leadership Development**. Between the ages of 30 and 40, the successor's plans stretch beyond any one job to the time when he or she will be responsible for the entire business. At this stage, the successor may develop skills of team-building and shared decision-making. If more than one successor candidate exists, this also may be the period when a natural leader emerges and self-selection occurs, as discussed in the first booklet of this series, *Family Business Succession: The Final Test of Greatness.*

5. **Selection.** If multiple candidates exist, selection should occur at this stage or sooner. As discussed in booklet No. 1 of The Family Business Leadership Series, a choice can be made in any of several ways, ranging from an early choice by the incumbent, to selection by the outside board or the family executive team, to consensus among family, board and executives.

6. **Transition.** This period, when authority and responsibility is transferred to the successor, also is covered in the first booklet. This may be the time when the successor gets involved in setting strategy and names his or her own management team.

7. **The Next Round.** Succession in the family business is a cyclical process that should never be neglected for long. Not long after transition, the business's new leaders should begin talking about developing the next generation of leaders.

Another kind of hero is a successor who is prepared to reinterpret tradition and make it valid as a living experience.

EXHIBIT 1

The Seven Stages of Successor Development

Stage 1.   ATTITUDE PREPARATION: Age 0-25. Development of key attitudes toward the family business and preparation through education and outside experience.

**Stage 2.   ENTRY: Age 20-30. Entry into the business, including training and orientation.

**Stage 3.   BUSINESS DEVELOPMENT: Age 25-35. Successor acquires needed business skills and experience.

**Stage 4.   LEADERSHIP DEVELOPMENT: Age 30-40. Successor acquires needed leadership skills and experience.

*Stage 5.   SELECTION: If multiple candidates exist, selection of a successor might occur at this stage or sooner.

*Stage 6.   TRANSITION: The transition to greater authority and responsibility.

Stage 7.   THE NEXT ROUND: Age 45 and up. Planning for the next round of succession.

*These stages are the focus of the first booklet in **The Family Business Leadership Series,** *Family Business Succession: The Final Test of Greatness.*

**These stages are the focus of this booklet.

Attitude Preparation:
The Early Years

Almost every family business leader beyond the first generation has vivid memories of how the family business affected his or her childhood.

One may remember sweeping the floors of the supply room, listening to the easy talk of employees. Another may have tucked in a drawer a tattered photo of himself as a child perched on a piece of heavy equipment, a parent smiling proudly nearby. Another recalls playing near an idle assembly line on a Sunday afternoon while his father worked in an office nearby.

Preparation of a family business successor does not begin when the incumbent leader starts to plan retirement. **Preparation is a lifelong process** that starts as soon as the child becomes conscious of the activities of the adults around him. **Work habits, attitudes toward the business, values and relationships all take root in the soil of childhood** and are formed over the years, long before successor development begins in any formal way.

Though nurturing young children for leadership is beyond the scope of this booklet, some concepts basic to the attitude preparation stage can be helpful in framing a personal development plan for the adult successor as well.

The Importance of Childhood Experience. Providing a home environment where a child experiences a sense of security and respect will best enable him or her to grow and develop individuality. Childhood experiences that instill family values are a crucial element of successor preparation as well.

For three generations, owners of Parisian, a chain of specialty retail stores based in Birmingham, Ala., have "learned the business at the family dinner table," says Donald Hess, who succeeded his father and grandfather as president. He describes the foundation of the family business as "generosity, respect for human values, sensitivity to the feelings of others, and commitment and dedication to improving the quality of life" for customers, vendors and employees. The result has been successful growth, excellent service and a low turnover rate among employees.

When fourth-generation members of the Sulzberger family, which controls the New York Times Co., were growing up, the family frequently convened at Hillendale, a family-owned estate in Connecticut.

There, the family heritage "was lightly but constantly present," one family member says.

Work habits are acquired by performing chores that contribute to the household, such as mowing lawns or babysitting. Children develop leadership and teamwork skills through activities such as scouting and sports. They learn accountability and self-reliance when they are given opportunities to make mistakes, create choices for themselves and see themselves as others see them.

Parents also can convey values and attitudes to their children by example. They may assume leadership posts in community organizations. Some take responsibility for helping the poor. Others encourage an enterprising approach to problems of all kinds, showing their offspring how to "create something from nothing."

Children also receive a powerful message from parents who achieve balance in their own lives between having fun and enjoying work. **Healthy attitudes toward the business spring from the enthusiasm and joy parents display in accomplishment, hard work, responsibility and sacrifice.**

Communicating About the Child's Future Role. The tone of any early discussions about the family business might be, "This work is exciting and worthwhile, and you may want to consider it when deciding what to do with your life." Key ideas to communicate are that the child is welcome in the family business, that his or her **participation is voluntary** and that the parent will support the child in any decision he or she makes. The possibility of "being the boss someday" probably shouldn't be raised until the child enters college or later. And it shouldn't be presented as a certainty. Rather than conveying a sense of entitlement, the parent should communicate the need for commitment, hard work and a sense of responsibility.

The Importance of Education. "Education" for the family business successor should not be defined simply as an MBA nor any other particular degree or diploma. Rather, it should be viewed as a lifelong process.

A college education may not be essential for every successor. Sometimes, honing skills within the business and keeping abreast of trends through industry seminars and trade gatherings can be sound preparation for succession. Leadership can be exercised through trade association meetings and conventions.

A college education can, however, offer opportunities to develop important skills as well as formal disciplines such as finance and marketing. The seven skills of leadership, writing and communication,

EXHIBIT 2 ███████████████████████████████████████

Laying the Psychological Groundwork for Success

Family business CEOs who feel they were well-prepared for their role tend to have had the following experiences, according to Bleke & Boyd, P.C., Atlanta-based management psychologists:

- A family environment in which they felt loved, secure and important.
- A realistic view of work and responsibility, with chores assigned and allowances earned.
- Opportunities to talk with parents about careers and education.
- Parents who actively offered counsel but did so without a heavy hand.
- Parents who encouraged discussion about career choices and planning for entry into the family business.
- An opportunity to "prove themselves" outside the family business before entering.

---

planning and organization, gathering information, solving problems, making decisions and exercising creativity are critical general management abilities and can be developed throughout school.

If the successor does decide to attend college, many parents raise questions that will help him or her begin setting developmental goals beyond choosing the "right" major or fraternity. What are the purposes of the college years? Are they a time to sow wild oats? To learn how to live independently? To manage one's time? To interact with good thinkers? To gain new life experiences? To choose a mate who can share or support your goals? Such questions can encourage a young person to think about personal objectives in broad terms.

The Value of Outside Experience. Psychologists say one of the most common problems facing family business successors is a sense of inertia. They may be reluctant or afraid to venture into the outside world. They may not feel they have any real choices about their career. They may feel they lack either the freedom or the ability to compete in the outside world. These feelings can be enervating and even disabling, leading to a lifetime of frustration.

A powerful antidote is experience in an outside job. **Most family business advisors strongly recommend that successors get three to five years of work experience outside the family business.** This gives the successor a chance to hear honest feedback, to be judged on his or her merits and to learn different approaches to management.

Outside experience gives the successor an opportunity to make youthful mistakes on someone else's turf, where he or she is just another employee — not an heir to the throne. The successor also learns that all bosses are not like Dad — they are often worse. An understanding that the grass is not always greener on the other side of the fence can be invaluable in securing the successor's commitment through tough times.

In all of our research, no one who worked outside the family business regretted doing so. Many who did not wished that they had. Encouraging successors to get outside experience can, however, foster a certain tension.

Andé Evers, founder of a Georgia maker of custom vehicles, wanted his son Tom to earn his own business credentials before joining the family business. Tom wasn't very interested in the family company at that point, and went on to score some major successes in sales for a large business-products concern.

When Andé asked Tom to join the family firm six years later, his son turned him down. "At that point, I was having fun and I had lots of opportunities," Tom says. Andé took the rejection as a challenge and set about changing Tom's mind. "My incentive was to grow this company to the point where it would be interesting to my son," he says. After two years of growth of the family business and intense father-son discussions, Tom returned as heir apparent in what father and son agree was "a business decision."

For all its value, some successors don't have a chance to acquire outside experience; they may be called home from college when the incumbent falls ill or dies. Others may acquire similar experience inside the family business if it is big enough, perhaps by being groomed in various divisions by nonfamily executives.

If the successor does stay close to home, special care should be taken to help him or her develop leadership, empathy for co-workers and an understanding of the stresses on supervisors. This can be accomplished through personal development planning, as discussed later. The successor should also take time to visit people at other businesses, to continue education and to be active in civic, trade and professional groups.

Entry Into the Business

Time spent at the family business as a child, or summer jobs as a teenager, can give the successor valuable work experience and insight into its culture and people. But when he or she reaches the age when permanent job decisions are made, new rules come into play.

Make Me An Offer. **A potential successor should enter the family business in response to a specific, formal offer to fill a job that is needed.** Pay and performance standards should be clear. This sets the stage for a businesslike, mutually respectful relationship between the successor and others in the business. It also means other employees who may doubt the successor's qualifications are less likely to feel resentful.

Many families shape successors' expectations by setting policies early for family participation in the business and enforcing them fairly. The policy may·define when and how family members become eligible for employment and, in some cases, what level of commitment they must make. The rules should be communicated clearly. They act as an agreement between parents and their offspring.

Once a job offer has been made, the decision to enter the business should be regarded as an important personal choice for the successor. He or she should not feel pressured or compelled. No decision should be taken as irrevocable. And the successor should be able to weigh the offer independent of any family coercion. **Without freedom to choose, the potential successor is less likely to make a strong commitment to the family business.**

The decision to commit to the family firm marks a turning point for the successor. At first glance, a job in the family business may seem like an easy route. In the long run, it probably will be harder than taking a job elsewhere. Family businesses can be difficult to run, according to noted organizational psychologist Harry Levinson, particularly if family feelings or traditions interfere with management. To succeed, the successor not only will have to emerge from the family's shadow and earn the respect of others involved with the business, but acquire important business and leadership skills. If the successor fails to make a contribution, he or she may be strongly resented by others in the business. And if relationships among family members are strained, entering the business can add new stress.

From the business owner's perspective, **a successor may need time**

and space to decide whether to join the company. Though incumbent leaders may be anxious themselves about the successor's decision, it is imperative to remember that the choice can be an agonizing, soul-searching one for a young successor. Many factors must be considered, including some that have nothing to do with the family or the parent-child relationship. The wisest and most compassionate thing the business owner can do, once the offer has been made, is to leave the decision completely to the successor.

Where to Begin? Some business owners have successors start in entry-level positions, while others bring them into the company later, in more responsible jobs that afford greater power and a shorter rise to the top. There are advantages and disadvantages to each approach, as discussed by Jeffrey A. Barach and others in the *Journal of Small Business Management* (April 1988, reprinted in *The Family Business Sourcebook*, Omnigraphics Inc., 1991).

A low-level starting point gives the successor a chance to become very familiar with the business and its employees, and to acquire specific skills. It gives the successor a chance to earn broad credibility among employees.

The late Dr. Ken Lipke didn't demand outside experience or college degrees of his five children when they entered the family steel sales and manufacturing business. But they began in low-level jobs as "go-fers," moving from department to department where needed. "As go-fers, they did all the tough jobs no one else wanted to do. And as Lipkes, they had to work twice as hard to prove themselves," Lipke said. Each gained broad knowledge of every department in the company. As a result, Lipke said, "my children are all excellent specialists with a good sense of the general."

Starting at the bottom has disadvantages as well. Normal mistakes may be viewed by employees and others with a hypercritical eye, as signs of incompetence. The successor may develop too narrow an understanding of the business environment. And the business owner may have even greater difficulty teaching or relinquishing control to a successor who, it may seem, only yesterday was just a "go-fer."

Bringing the successor into the organization later, at a higher level, such as upper-middle or top management, can encourage him or her to gain experience, self-confidence and growth independent of the family business. It affords the successor a broader perspective of the business environment. And it encourages family business insiders to judge the successor's skills with greater objectivity.

On the other hand, the successor who starts near the top may lack

EXHIBIT 3 ▐█████████████████████████████████████

What Should I Consider Before Joining the Business?

- What are the reasons for my decision?
- Does it offer the career I want?
- Does it fulfill my personal goals?
- Do I like what the business does?
- Will I find the work meaningful and challenging?
- Is it better than my alternatives?
- Can I work with my family?
- Can I make a real contribution?
- What skill, talent, drive and knowledge can I bring to the business?
- Can we resolve conflicts that will inevitably arise?
- Do I understand that being a "good son or daughter" is different from being an effective manager?

---

specific expertise and skills needed in running the family business. He or she may face resentment from long-term employees who see the successor advanced ahead of them. And the successor's work and management habits acquired outside the family business may conflict with the family business culture.

Wherever successors start out, they should know from the beginning where they stand. If leading the business is a possibility but not a promise, the successor should be told. Similarly, each should know what criteria must be met before he or she will be asked to take over. This can be accomplished in the process of planning for the successor's personal development, as discussed in the next section.

The Business Development Stage

The successor will need, usually between the ages of about 25 to 35, to develop basic business skills as a foundation for future leadership. Let's take a look at some elements of planning for this period of intense personal growth.

The Personal Development Plan. A personal development plan is a road map describing the skills and attributes the successor already has, the skills that need developing, a program for acquiring them and a means for measuring progress.

To entrepreneurs or others who have never had one, a personal development plan may seem unnecessary. But it can be crucial in helping successors stay the course. First, it acts as a yardstick for accomplishment, allowing the successor to take satisfaction in his or her progress. Second, it can help the successor keep an eye on long-term goals in the face of short-term setbacks. And third, it increases the likelihood that the successor actually will develop the kind of leadership skills that will be needed in the future.

The plan should lay out a developmental program, a kind of master plan of activities. It will identify roles and jobs within the company to support the successor's development — from warehouse supervisor to assistant regional sales manager to head of a new-systems task force. Each step should be congruent with the needs of the business.

Part of this process is to envision the likely future shape and requirements of the company, based on its strategic plan. Will the family business require a superb salesperson to lead it into the future? Will new product development be the key to future success? Or will astute financial management make the difference? These are the kinds of questions incumbent leaders must ask themselves in helping map the successor's developmental path.

The personal development plan may also set goals of acquiring attributes important to good leadership. Attitudes, for instance, are fundamental. **Assuming responsibility for oneself, giving customers first priority, exercising initiative and stewardship in managing assets, and cultivating commitment to the family business are attitudes often found in outstanding leaders.** These can also serve as specific criteria by which successors can be evaluated. Skill development is next in importance, including leadership, communications and analytical skills.

Specific knowledge, including an understanding of business processes and industry trends, follows in importance.

Ideally, the plan should provide for running a profit center, building one's own organization, setting goals with outside review, working with a mentor and finding peer groups and models. The plan also should identify resources available to meet the successor's developmental needs. Something as simple as planning when and how to include the successor in the flow of corporation information — board minutes, financial reports, planning memos and the like — can help the successor learn faster about all areas of the business.

The plan also might discuss achieving community-leadership roles. It could lay out a reading list of books and periodicals to support gaining knowledge and skill. It might describe ways of developing a network of potential business contacts.

No matter how painstaking the planning process, it should be clear throughout that the successor is ultimately responsible for his or her development. Any personal development plan is designed only to give potential successors the maximum opportunity to develop themselves to their full potential. It offers no guarantees.

How Do Successors Learn? A common error by family business owners is to assume that successors will learn what they need to know automatically, by osmosis or casual contact. While some learning takes place that way, it is usually insufficient to fully develop the successor's potential or instill the kind of leadership skills that will be necessary in the future.

Successors are more likely to reach their full potential through doing and through organized communication and work with mentors, peers and industry contacts who can share experience and insight. These learning opportunities don't just happen in a family business. They must be planned. If a successor's career path is dictated by chance, zigzagging here and there through jobs that happen to open up, he or she has far less chance of acquiring the broad, challenging experience that makes for a great leader. **An effective successor development plan strikes a balance between meeting the**

No matter how painstaking the planning process, it should be clear throughout that the successor is ultimately responsible for his or her development.

EXHIBIT 4

A Sampling of Important Developmental Experiences

- Identifying and expressing values.
- Determining how values can be manifested in the business.
- Turning an operation around.
- Having failures and dealing with them.
- Having a lousy job and coping well.
- Starting from scratch.
- Handling a subordinate's performance problems.
- Breaking out of a rut.
- Moving from line to staff and back again.
- Being demoted.
- Being unwisely promoted.
- Building something from nothing.
- Dealing with personal traumas.
- Identifying appropriate role models.
- Stabilizing a failing operation.
- Striking out in new directions.

needs of the business while giving the successor a wide range of challenges, experiences and opportunities.

Throughout these experiences, the successor will pass milestones that won't be marked on anyone's plan or organization chart. These are the developmental experiences from the "school of hard knocks" — the events that can't be planned or predicted, but that taken together create a seasoned executive with sound judgment.

Getting Started. Ideally, the successor should participate in writing the personal development plan based on what he or she is learning about his or her developmental needs. A mentor or coach can help, with oversight by incumbent leaders and an outside board, if one exists. **The successor might begin with such questions as, "Where am I, in terms of**

my personal and business development?" and, "How do I plan to develop needed skills in the coming years?"

If getting started is difficult, outside sources can often help. One successor recalls being unhappy and frustrated a few years into his work in the family business because he, his brother and father weren't communicating about the future of the business. Though the father had said he would retire in eight years, the elder son didn't feel either he or his brother were being prepared to take over.

At the elder son's suggestion, all three men attended family business seminars and programs aimed at smoothing succession. Aptitude testing suggested by a seminar leader showed the elder son that he had some abilities he did not know he had, including systems management and marketing. After his father saw the test results, the two had a starting point and it was easy for them to sit down and begin talking about personal development.

Developing Complementary Skills. Even at this early stage, successors should plan to structure their skills to avoid areas where the parent already is strong. The successor's target skills should *complement* rather than *compete with* those of the boss. This not only fortifies management in weak areas, but helps avoid conflict and direct comparison with the parent. If the parent is strong in operations but weak in record-keeping, the successor might plan to develop accounting and information-systems expertise. If the parent is a master salesperson but weak at administration, the successor might hone organizational and communications skills.

Perhaps the family business's current generation of leaders has run their operation informally, shunning inventory control, market research, forecasting, cost accounting and other formal business practices. Such deficiencies provide fertile fields for the next generation to make its mark by improving management. Other successors make a valuable contribution through "external thinking" — exploring the market for clues to future growth and profit.

Measuring Progress. The successor and a mentor or coach should continually set performance goals that can be measured. This is crucial, since the definition of "a job well done" can be highly subjective — especially when strong family feelings are involved. Goals should be specific. Some examples: hire a salesman during the second quarter; buy and install new equipment by the end of the year; design a preventive maintenance program; attend two management seminars a year; analyze employee productivity; analyze new-product performance.

As the successor progresses to the leadership development stage, goals may include a range of accomplishments critical to the business: a demonstrated ability to handle profit-and-loss responsibility; dealing appropriately with a flagging operation; negotiating an acquisition or divestiture; success with difficult personnel problems; managing external relationships with customers, clients or professional advisors; managing complex financial transactions; handling purchasing responsibility; or negotiating a union contract.

The plan should describe how and when the successor and mentor or coach will regularly review progress. Supervisors should be familiar with the developmental plan and help measure the successor's progress. Ideally, successors' goals also should be shared with trusted and qualified outsiders, such as directors, accountants, lawyers or consultants.

Peers can help monitor and encourage progress too. At one medium-sized family business, four members of the next generation of management report to each other on their progress against their personal development plans. These cousins gather, usually annually, so each can present an assessment of his or her personal development needs and a plan on how to address them. "I need to develop better people skills," one cousin might report. Another said, "I need to become more verbal and expressive." A third wanted to develop better organizational skills.

After the meeting, the cousins do some individual work on ways each might help others attain needed skills, based on their role in the business. A few weeks later, the same group meets again, and each cousin offers ideas on "Here's how I think I can help you." This not only builds team spirit, but it fosters a sense of freedom among the cousins in disclosing needs and weaknesses. A facilitator, such as a trusted advisor or consultant, can be helpful at such meetings, especially when getting started.

The Role of Mentors. Pairing up with a personal mentor for three to five years can be invaluable to a successor.

A mentor's job, in part, is to help the successor learn to exercise judgment, take risks, accept a philosophical commitment to sharing and relate to people in an empathetic and intuitive way. The mentor also may confer specific business knowledge, particularly if he or she is skilled in areas the successor wants to develop.

A primary qualification of a mentor is a keen regard for the successor's best interests and a desire to help the successor become even more successful than the mentor. The mentor must be someone who would never feel threatened by even the wildest success on the part of the successor.

The mentor should not be the successor's parent or boss, however. This frees the successor to ask difficult questions or to appear vulnerable.

Ideally, the mentor will be a trusted professional advisor or outside director who knows the business, the family and the successor well. Under the best circumstances, this will be a confidential relationship that exists only for the benefit of the successor — not a vehicle for channeling information about the successor to a parent or boss.

Mentoring relationships should be informal and based on personal affinity. In the most successful mentoring relationships, the successor takes most of the responsibility for initiating contact. Every few weeks, he or she should find a reason to sit down with the mentor with an informal agenda in mind. "These are the kinds of things I'd like to talk about," the successor might say. "Why do we price our product this way?" or "Why was this idea of mine rejected?" or "Where is the industry going?" might be starting points.

If the mentor is an outside director, the successor might visit his or her business, learning about management systems, human resources or other aspects of professional management. One director of a family foods concern occasionally stops at the company on his way home from work to talk to the owner's sons about any problems they may have. The director offered advice when one of the sons wanted to open retail units in department stores. "We had no idea how a department store works, but this director did," the owner says. The director helped the son prepare pro forma financial statements and organize the units.

Some successors benefit from having two mentors. One may be someone with knowledge and experience in the successor's job area, who helps the successor become proficient on the job. The other mentor watches "the big picture," guiding the successor along a career path and helping focus his or her thinking about the future. This "career path" mentor is always on the lookout for opportunities for the successor, and helps him or her evaluate and act upon them when they do arise.

Successors also should be encouraged to seek out models in the business or community whom they admire and want to emulate. While relationships with a model are more distant than with a mentor, they nevertheless can provide valuable counsel and inspiration.

The Role of Other Trusted Outsiders. Directors, industrial psychologists and consultants also can play uniquely helpful roles in successor development.

Directors: If your family business has an active outside board, a director or a committee of the board can be given responsibility for monitoring and guiding successor development. Early in the process, directors can help develop the criteria for future top management, based on the direction of strategy and the industry.

Once successors are working in the business, the board can help set successors' compensation and monitor their learning opportunities. Often, directors discover that successors are not being challenged enough — that they need to be thrown in over their heads to develop skills and discover the depth of their capabilities. The board can help suggest new challenges.

Interaction with directors can be a valuable learning experience. The successor might be asked to give reports to the board and hear directors' feedback. Directors also can help simply by showing interest in his or her work and talking about their own experiences.

Eventually, the successor can become a member of the board as part of the transition to leadership.

The board also can be a vehicle for contact with other outsiders. Some family businesses name directors from the successor's peer group as role models. Directors can provide a network of business leaders and other successors to act as role models.

Directors also can help communicate successor-development plans to shareholders. This can be a challenge, particularly if inactive shareholders underestimate the importance of preparing for leadership. If questions arise about whether successor development is necessary or why so many resources are being expended on so few, directors, as impartial advisors, can be helpful in clarifying goals and clearing up misunderstandings.

Industrial Psychologist: Few successors can make fast progress without a developmental tool that is in short supply in many family businesses: an unbiased and skilled reflection of his or her strengths and weaknesses. The most obvious person to offer such feedback — the parent — is also often the least effective. A director, immediate supervisor or another family member can provide some helpful feedback, but they may lack the skill, objectivity and insight needed to do a thorough job.

An industrial psychologist may be the best candidate. Once the successor's strengths and weaknesses have been identified, the industrial psychologist can communicate and help analyze them, as well as lay plans for developing them.

Most family businesses who employ an industrial psychologist in successor development do not have him or her report to the boss or parents. The relationship with the successor should be a positive and confidential one, enabling the psychologist to offer coaching, insights and advice free of judgments or directives from the parent. Openness and vulnerability are essential to uncovering and addressing weaknesses. And

EXHIBIT 5 ███████████████████████████████████████

How Directors Can
Aid Successor Development

- Monitor the overall process
- Help develop criteria for future top management
- Help set compensation of successors
- Monitor successor's learning opportunities
- Suggest new challenges for the successor
- Provide potential outside business contacts or role models
- Act individually as mentors to the successor
- Hear formal reports from the successor and give feedback
- Provide peer-group role models of entrepreneurship and leadership
- Help communicate succession process and plans to family members
- Assist in selecting a new business leader

---

the successor is far more likely to be open, disclosing and vulnerable to a professional whose job is to keep confidences, than to a parent or boss. The message to the successor should be, "You're not on trial here. I'm here as a resource to you."

Once the successor has named his or her weaknesses with the help of a supportive coach, he or she is ready to tackle them on the job. The successor is also far more likely to have the courage and confidence to say to a supervisor, "I need to develop in these areas. How can I best do that? Can you provide me experiences on the job that will help me, and offer feedback to help measure my progress?"

If more than one successor is competing for a top job, an industrial psychologist can be particularly helpful in shaping each candidate's expectations. Clashes often arise because candidates' self-images are out of line with reality. An industrial psychologist can help each understand personal strengths and weaknesses in a nonjudgmental atmosphere and understand how far he or she is likely to progress in management. This can allay potential conflict among successors and greatly smooth the succession process.

Consultant: Many family businesses tap an organizational consultant or university professor to help with successor development, particularly if intensive training in a technical area is needed. This person might, for instance, hone the successor's knowledge and skills in the area of finance and help him or her apply those techniques within the business.

Learning about Strategy, History and Culture. Successors should spend significant time learning the history of the business, though it should not become a full-time job. The focus should be on key strategic issues and events, why decisions were made as they were and what lessons were learned in the process.

Some families ask successors to compile a history of the family business, if one doesn't exist already. The successor also may be asked to write a culture statement. These exercises accomplish two purposes. They make explicit the company history and culture, which typically are only implicit in the day-to-day life of a business. And the successor learns a great deal about the business in the process of writing them down.

Some families also ask the successor to write a statement of the business's strategy. This doesn't mean that the successor is allowed to create or direct strategy. But writing down perceptions of strategy and getting reactions from key people in the business can be a valuable exercise in understanding it. It can prepare the successor for thinking beyond day-to-day operations to more abstract issues — a crucial step in learning to plan strategy.

Involvement in Business Processes and Ceremonies. Many family businesses have successors witness such important business processes as board meetings or strategic planning sessions. This allows them to observe shared decision-making and learn about complex issues. There is a risk, however, in inviting successors to these gatherings too early. He or she may feel so uncomfortable and out of place that it is impossible to learn. Sending the successor written minutes can be a good alternative.

Company socials and ceremonies, such as the employee-of-the-year award or a plant opening, can be valuable learning experiences as well. These allow the successor to absorb some culture and history while observing employees and other family members in non-routine situations.

The Importance of Outside Activities. Outside development activities should continue while the successor is working in the family business. Peer, civic or other groups and industry associations and seminars can aid in both personal development and acquiring specific knowledge.

Holding an officership or leadership role in an industry association can be valuable. Some families find it wise to limit the successor's outside activities to a maximum of two to three organizations or associations.

Ideally, successors should attend at least two industry or personal-development seminars each year, including one week-long workshop and a shorter gathering lasting one to three days. Travel can be a valuable learning tool as well. Visits to other family businesses is one technique with tremendous potential impact. These trips can be set up by a mentor, director or advisor and can be reciprocal for family businesses at similar stages in the succession process. The successor gets to observe the dynamics and culture of another family business, talk with other family business presidents and successors, and learn from the comparisons and contrasts that will arise.

One objective in planning these visits might be to **expose the successor to the real futurists in a relevant industry or field of expertise** — those who tend to lead change or to innovate successfully. This concept, often called "**benchmarking**," sets as a standard the capabilities of the top performer. This can be valuable in helping the successor think beyond conventional approaches to broadening markets, anticipating unusual potential competitors and seeing different applications for the products the family business makes. These experiences will encourage the successor to ask, "What are the skills we need, the talents we must develop, the moves our company must make, in order to succeed? And who are the best companies or people in each activity right now?"

Benchmark performers need not be in your own industry. An industrial laundry business, for instance, might take lessons from Federal Express in running an efficient pick-up and delivery network and keeping track of inventory. An industrial pump maker might study the sales capabilities of Xerox or another successful hard-goods vendor. Whatever the parallels, the underlying theme of these pursuits is continually to stretch the boundaries of the successor's thinking and encourage him or her to go beyond conventional wisdom.

The Leadership Development Stage

Once the successor has acquired some basic business skills, he or she can move on to developing the capabilities and qualities associated with leadership. The successor's focus at this stage stretches beyond the present to the time when he or she will be responsible for the entire business.

Earning Legitimacy. The distinction between power and authority is subtle but important. Power is the capacity to influence the behavior of others, while authority is the extent to which a person's power is viewed as legitimate.

Successors in family businesses often have power as a result of being members of the family that owns the business, but they may lack the authority needed to effectively manage the firm. Broad knowledge of the company's operations gained through experience, proven success in another company, community leadership and a thorough understanding of customer needs are all qualifications that can give the successor legitimacy in the eyes of employees and other stakeholders and lend the authority he or she needs to be an effective manager, according to Yale University's Dr. Ivan Lansberg, a noted family business consultant.

No matter how the successor enters the family business, it takes time to earn authority. A study by Jeffrey Barach and others (*Journal of Small Business Management*, April 1988) showed that the successors surveyed took an average of five years to win the respect of employees, or as little as two years if the successor implemented some successful innovations. For instance, one successor restored financial order in the family business by applying basic cost-accounting procedures, while another saved a major unit of the business by implementing simple marketing techniques.

One way to ensure that the successor will earn authority within the organization is to increase his or her responsibility step by step and to award new duties only after current ones have been mastered. First, a successor must demonstrate an ability to assume responsibility for himself or herself. The next step is supervising others. Budget duties may come next, followed by responsibility for increasing profitability. If promotions are based on accomplishment, the successor will have an opportunity to earn great internal credibility.

Some companies make mastery of new skills part of a contract whereby the successor gradually assumes control. After several years' outside experience, the successor at a family-held maker of custom vehicles joined the company as sales and marketing manager. He is taking over other areas of responsibility one-by-one, moving on only after he and the company's board of directors agree that he has mastered each new area. Once all departments report to the successor, he automatically becomes chief operating officer. And when he finally assumes responsibility for overseeing outside business contacts, including accountants, lawyers and consultants, he becomes chief executive officer.

Ideally, successors should move through jobs within several different functions of the business. A CEO candidate probably should not spend his or her entire career in a single area, such as sales or production, for instance. He or she should spend some time in at least one other key function, such as finance or retail sales, before moving up.

At The New York Times Co., Arthur Ochs Sulzberger Jr. succeeded his father as publisher of the flagship, *The New York Times*, only after he had several years' outside experience and had held at least nine other jobs inside the company, including reporter, advertising salesman, night production manager and corporate planner. He still reports to his father, Arthur Ochs Sulzberger Sr., who is chairman and CEO of the company.

Throughout this process, the successor gradually assumes more hiring and firing responsibility. Some family businesses actually have the successor assemble his or her own management team during the rise through the ranks, building into management some redundancy during transition. While the predecessor's management team stays in place, the successor is simultaneously grooming replacements for each member when they retire.

If incumbent leaders decide to have the successor wait until positions open up through attrition, the successor nevertheless can prepare to assemble his or her own management team by collecting resumes, gathering business cards and learning what salaries will be required to attract key recruits.

Creating New Positions. Creating a new position for the successor is rarely a good idea, particularly when he or she first joins the business permanently. This should be done only when the needs of the business require it — not because the successor needs a place to park.

Often, it **is** necessary to broaden the management team at some point. You may need to create new vice presidencies of marketing, finance and operations, for instance, to aid in revitalizing strategy, managing growth or coping with industry change. New staff positions may be needed for quality management or a systems overhaul. If people in the business have already identified a new function as necessary, and if the successor is qualified, then creating a post for him or her is fine.

Another kind of management change can be appropriate. **As the transition to new leadership approaches, some incumbents begin molding the top three or four executives, including the successor, into a team. As this group learns how to share decisionmaking, the successor may emerge as a natural leader.** If that occurs, the successor's step up to the presidency is a self-evident one, and a new position — chairman of the board — can be created for the incumbent.

The New Profit Center. Some family businesses organize a new profit center and put the successor in charge. This can be done with existing operations, providing there is a good business reason. Family owners of one business that had long been structured around the functions of sales, operations, finance and administration decided that the business had grown enough to split it into two geographic divisions. This permitted tighter integration of functions, as well as offering two talented successors each a chance to act as general manager of a partially autonomous business.

Another family business gave each of two talented successors two jobs. Each was responsible for his own profit center. Each also ran a division of the corporation, managing all the functions involved. This had the dual advantage of giving each successor hands-on operating experience without bumping aside key nonfamily executives with the divisions who were already running their own parts of the business.

Another family put a successor in charge of integrating an acquisition into the existing business. This involved shutting down a plant and overhauling systems of the acquired concern, and it provided a rich and rare developmental opportunity for the heir-apparent.

The New Venture. A successor also might be put in charge of an entirely new venture. A successor in a meatpacking business was allowed to field a frozen hamburger to a new institutional market, for instance. A successor in a fresh-fish retailer might be allowed to try to take a frozen product national under the family's brand name.

Though this can be a valuable step in the successor's development, it has some drawbacks. If the profit center is a startup, everyone involved should understand the special hazards from the outset. First, new ventures are risky and usually don't turn out as planned; everyone involved should be encouraged to have realistic expectations. Second, the successor may need greater flexibility, resources and time to make it work than is apparent at the outset. Third, **limits should be set in advance for**

time and money that will be spent on the new venture. Fourth, the successor should not be evaluated solely on the success or failure of a startup. Rather, it should be viewed as an important but risky part of the successor development process, as well as a strategic learning experience for the company.

The Balancing Act. Making moves of the kind described above often requires tradeoffs. The opportunities and needs that exist in the business must be reconciled with the successor's needs and interests.

The successor may need experience as general manager of a profit center, but the business may need him or her right now on the plant floor. The successor may need to attend an industry seminar, but the business may need him or her to put out a fire in accounting. In smaller businesses, it can be particularly tough to align the successor's need for time to learn with the demands of running the business.

How much should you shape the family business to accommodate the talents and developmental needs of the successor? And how much should you stretch the successor to meet the needs of the family business as currently structured? These pressures sometimes inspire clever and creative ideas for accommodating the needs of both the successor and the business. In other cases, the only answer is to set aside the successor's development temporarily until pressures ease or new opportunities arise in the business. This is one reason it is helpful to begin the successor-development process early. When imperatives collide, sometimes the only sensible solution is to delay one or the other.

Another aspect of the balancing act is the question of whether to play to a successor's strengths or to work on his or her weaknesses. Developmental efforts related to the successor's weaknesses should not turn deficiencies into stigmas. An introverted and shy successor, for instance, should not be forced to become head of sales. A preferable course might be to leave the person in production or another area where he or she is strong, while developing people skills in other ways such as Toastmasters Club or Dale Carnegie courses. (Please see the Resources List at the end of this booklet.) That might be combined with some business activity that requires occasional calls on customers without the make-or-break pressure of sales.

Maintaining objectivity on these issues is often difficult for family business owners. An outside board can be helpful in striking the right balance.

Holding Two Jobs at Once. Many family businesses find it helpful for successors to hold two jobs. They should hold a position in the business

EXHIBIT 6 ▰▰▰▰▰▰▰▰▰▰▰▰▰▰▰▰▰▰▰▰▰▰▰▰

Trade-Offs in
Successor Development

- Developing the successor's weaknesses vs. playing to strengths
- Developing skills through outside activities vs. getting a job done in the business
- Developing breadth of experience vs. depth of specialized knowledge
- Preserving tradition vs. embracing change
- Bottom-up career path vs. starting at the top
- Pay according to the job filled vs. pay according to qualifications and education
- Treat like everyone else vs. offer special experiences for future ownership and leadership
- Spoon-feed knowledge vs. "throw them to the wolves"
- "Work your way up" vs. planned moves to successively more challenging jobs
- Diverse experience for successor vs. protecting incumbent nonfamily managers
- Encouraging new approaches vs. grounding in basic skills and practices
- Meeting the needs of the successor vs. meeting the needs of the business
- Serving the conservatism of the maturing family business vs. the entrepreneurial spirit and innovation required of successors.
- Balancing the older generation's need for stability and control vs. successors' need for change and freedom.
- Preserving the legend of the entrepreneur as hero vs. cultivating a team approach in later generations of management.

---

accomplishing something each day and turning in measurable results.

At the same time, successors should have some kind of task-force responsibility that cuts across the many functions of the business. These broader duties immerse the successor in many parts of the business and bring him or her into contact with a wide range of people. Examples of responsibilities often assigned to task forces are listed in the following table.

EXHIBIT 7 ████████████████████████████████████

Task-Force Opportunities

- Lead strategic planning exercises
- Conduct an analysis of a key market
- Open or shut down a facility or plant
- Conduct due-diligence work on an acquisition
- Organize a total quality management program
- Develop and implement a performance review system
- Develop a compensation plan
- Build an employee benefits plan

Situations with Multiple Siblings

About half of all family businesses now employ multiple offspring, compared with one-fifth just a few years ago. That means successor development is often a group process, with candidates for various top jobs in the business proceeding along their own career paths toward a place on a new leadership team.

All of these successors should have the opportunity to follow a personal development program. Each should know the criteria for moving into top jobs. If appropriate, incumbent leaders may even define additional leadership roles for qualified candidates who may not be in line for existing slots.

The Team Approach. Often, **an entrepreneur who has been a one-person show throughout his career is succeeded by a team of managers.** Individual members of the team may lack the founder's breadth of knowledge and perhaps intensity of commitment (or obsession). Each may work 60 hours a week to the founder's ninety. But together, the team members can bring a depth of management that can equip the business for new frontiers of growth. In fact, the failure of any family business to assemble a team of managers by the third generation of family ownership should raise questions about whether the business is growing at a healthy rate.

If a team approach is planned, **the ability to work together as a team becomes a goal in successor development** — and a criterion for selection of the CEO. In a growing number of family businesses, the distinctions in status among members of the management team are small. While the CEO will be the team leader, all members will need similar nontechnical skills.

Some family businesses are taking team management one step further, by naming an executive committee of several children who serve in an "office of the president." Others rotate the presidency among the children.

Fostering Teamwork. A healthy family is the best starting point for fostering management teamwork. Children from healthy families tend to talk out conflicts and negotiate differences. Members listen to each other and weigh alternatives together. Because each member is heard,

31

respected and valued, each is willing to pull together with others without resentment or resistance.

Another building block is effective communication. Successors should be told, through the succession planning process or written policies, that the CEO's job is not the only important role in the success of the family business. Instead, qualified members of the next generation will have a range of opportunities to contribute to top management. While all career paths won't end up at the apex of the organization, individuals' contributions in other jobs are nevertheless valuable and crucial.

Other effective techniques are to appoint successors to task forces together or send them on business trips or other excursions as a group.

Teamwork can help siblings each enjoy greater developmental opportunities. In one family business, several members of the fourth generation have organized themselves to follow different career paths upward through the organization. Three of the young men each head sales and service in separate product areas. A fourth family member is planning to acquire skills in finance before entering the business. With some help, the group has created a developmental plan that will allow each brother to grow within the organization for 15 years before they will begin competing directly for the top job. By that time, they hope, they will have selected a leader themselves.

A team approach also can make possible a smooth transfer of power. As successors develop business skills, they can be made members of an "executive committee" of top management. Gradually, incumbent leaders can defer more decisions to the committee. All the members develop greater depth and breadth of skill, while successors have an opportunity to demonstrate good judgment and original ideas. Ideally, one successor candidate emerges as the natural leader of the team. By the time authority is actually transferred, this candidate is part of a smooth-functioning top-management team and can assume leadership without unnecessary drama or pressure.

Developing Multiple Candidates. Developing more than one successor candidate is often wise. This ensures that if one candidate is disqualified or becomes unavailable for any reason, the business owner won't have to start from scratch.

Also, many family businesses are led at different times by different members of the same generation. In many companies, the oldest member of the younger generation is too young to take the helm when the CEO is reaches retirement age or decides to retire early. A "bridge manager," sometimes an uncle, aunt or nonfamily executive, can take charge in such cases.

If the Shoe Fits...

Some business owners cherish a dream that a particular child will lead the business.

This dream may be shattered if the successor lacks the desire or affinity for top management. Rather than trying to mold these young people into something they do not want to be, it is usually better to encourage them to develop their talents and interests and follow their own personal development paths. In a newspaper family, one young man loved to work with the presses. Instead of forcing him to move into other areas of management, the family charted a career path for him that ended in the production manager's job.

Others may seek simply to exercise their craft. One entrepreneur who started her own communications consulting business was frustrated that her daughter lacked any desire to succeed her, but wanted only to expand the firm's computer graphics. "How do I change her?" the mother asked. Most likely, she cannot, without making the daughter very unhappy. The best remedy in this case is probably to allow her to develop the potential of the graphics side of the business to the fullest.

If the successor development process leaves the incumbent with no viable candidates for succession, he or she should recognize and accept that fact as early as possible. The next generation might still own the business, but professional management may be necessary. Or, the family may decide that continuing family ownership is neither appropriate nor in the best interests of the business and all who depend on it.

Nonfamily Candidates for Succession. If nonfamily candidates are considered, a few principles are worth noting. Ideally, a nonfamily CEO can be found within the business. Preferably, candidates should have three to five years' experience in the business before moving into the top job. If possible, the business owner should identify two candidates, allowing a period of preparation and evaluation before a final choice is made. Planning pays off under these circumstances. If the business owner has been cross-training nonfamily executives to develop a seasoned management team, identifying a nonfamily candidate for CEO will be far easier.

If no nonfamily candidate exists within the business, hiring a nonfamily candidate for the CEO job is an extremely risky alternative. Under these circumstances, the sale of the business might be considered.

The Role of the Successor
in Business Revitalization

No matter how powerful or compelling the vision of the entrepreneur, most express it only in bits and pieces. Entrepreneurs tend to depend upon their decisions and deeds, rather than words, to convey their vision to others.

The task of transforming the entrepreneurial vision into a shared mission that can inspire and empower others usually falls to successors. Typically, they are the first to interpret to others the meaning of the business's existence and survival. At the heart of this challenge lies an opportunity. In answering questions like, "Why are we so successful?" successors have a golden opportunity to manage the meaning of the company history and culture in a way that gives the business a competitive advantage and the family a sense of meaning and purpose.

Capitalizing on Culture. In the healthy family business, the wise successor will strive to retain the strengths of the culture while implementing needed changes.

In fact, **the best first step in implementing change in the family business may be preserving as much tradition as you can.** The successor's task is to build a desire for change into the existing tradition in a way that makes it seem that seeking change was always a part of the business's culture. That means respecting and promoting the corporate culture and valuing and repeating the legends, stories and traditions that help make the business unique.

This may require the successor to temper a natural desire to throw out completely the "old way" of doing things. As tempting as that may be, it wastes one of the most valuable assets of the family business: a sense of tradition and shared values. These feelings among family business shareholders and employees can foster a kind of consistency, loyalty and teamwork that is the envy of publicly-held competitors.

The Importance of Change. At the same time, one of the greatest enemies of any business is the idea that

> *The task of transforming the entrepreneurial vision into a shared mission that can inspire and empower others usually falls to successors.*

35

"the past is our master." Family businesses are particularly vulnerable. It may fall to the successor to shake off complacency. While the status quo may have worked fine for a long while, the accelerating rate of change in today's business environment will wipe out any companies that fail to adapt. Business leaders must find ways continually to revitalize both strategy and culture.

Bissell Inc., the family-owned household-products concern, endured for more than 50 years with a conservative one-product strategy, making carpet sweepers and distributing the profits to the family. But the third generation of family managers struck a new balance. Building on the strength and integrity of the Bissell name, they began diversifying into related new products, such as vacuum cleaners, and reinvesting profits in the business. They also shocked family members by encouraging family executives to leave the company to make way for highly qualified outsiders.

All the while, the new leaders guarded the company's well-recognized name and values and adhered to a Bissell tradition of taking special care of employees. While the founding generation had looked out for workers with progressive worker's compensation, disability and retirement plans, the new leaders offered stock to loyal, long-term employees.

By preserving this delicate equilibrium, Bissell "keeps the best of the old but stays vibrant and growing by remaining open to new ideas," says John M. Bissell, president.

How To Accomplish Change. A study of the business' history can be invaluable in implementing change. Often, a successor can reinterpret the business's past to stakeholders, emphasizing the ways in which critical challenges were overcome. If corporate legends are retold with an emphasis on the value of change, stakeholders will begin to see adaptability as an element of the **existing** culture.

Celebrating new ideas and presenting seeming threats as opportunities can all help lead the business toward adaptability. Uncle Henry, for instance, may have invented all the manufacturing equipment that enabled Smith Corp. to become the first mass producer of cream-filled doughnuts in the nation. If that story is retold with an emphasis on the creativity and resolve Uncle Henry demonstrated in persevering in a strategy few others believed would work, family members and employees will begin to see the value of innovation in the business.

Corporate slogans can be reworded in the same way. Instead of repeating, "A good salesman will deliver it himself," say, "A good salesperson finds solutions to a customer's problems." The new slogan preserves the traditional focus on service (as well as eliminating assumptions about gender), but stresses individual initiative and creativity rather than repetition of a specific activity.

Perhaps most important, **the successor must become an example of receptivity to change.** He or she must be flexible and open to improvements at every turn, providing a living example of how tradition can be preserved — and enriched — through change.

Revitalizing Strategy. Early in the successor's development, his or her main role regarding strategy is to learn about it — what it is, how it was made and how it has changed over time. Some families allow successors to audit strategic-planning sessions very early. As the successor gains experience, he or she may become involved in strategic planning by serving on a task force. Eventually, the successor becomes an agent of strategic change, sometimes even proposing a new strategy for the business to the CEO or the board.

Usually, strategic change is best accomplished gradually, without creating the impression that new approaches are being forced on the organization. It is best, for instance, to plant the seeds of new ideas, not fully formed conclusions. If possible, new approaches can be tested quietly, in small-scale experiments, then allowed to "sell themselves" through their results. Instead of announcing, "I've got an idea!" the successor might take a more low-key approach: "What do you think about (doing) such-and-such?" This method avoids setting up situations where people are pitted against each other over minor issues.

Finally, **new ideas must be allowed to blossom as others become supportive.** A proposed change can be legitimized through creation of a committee, and allies can be won through the naming of an internal "champion" who becomes closely associated with the success of the idea.

If a change in direction is necessary, the successor may become the person who communicates it to the family — with the clear support of the older generation. Strategy plays a vital role in securing the commitment of shareholders, particularly when ownership is dispersed among many family members. As the third-generation successor in one family business prepared to take over from his older cousin, he learned that family shareholders harbored doubts about his abilities. When an advisor urged him not to assume that he would automatically take charge in a few years when his cousin retired, the successor said, "Well, I guess

The successor must become an example of receptivity to change.

37

I'm going to have to sell myself to the family." A better way to look at the challenge would be that he needs to present a vision that the rest of the family can embrace.

The strategic vision for the business and the values that underlie it are pivotal in uniting shareholders and ensuring stability of the company's capital base. If the strategic vision is communicated well, in a way that responds to the goals and needs of shareholders, the successor has scored a major accomplishment.

Family Relations
During Successor Development

The entire family should be aware, in a general sense, of plans for successor development.

Regular communication can help educate family members on the requirements of a good leader. Keep them informed about how you are grooming and choosing someone, how the process is going and what your feelings are about it. Accept input as the process continues. This makes visible to the family the planning and work that goes into a fair and effective succession process. Also, you avoid alienating possible successors and seeming secretive.

Inactive shareholders, in particular, need to understand the importance of preparing the next generation for the heavy demands of leadership. These are usually underappreciated. To them, career planning may seem like a special privilege, but it is essential for strong management — and common to all well-run companies.

The way you introduce the concept of successor development depends in part on your philosophy of managing the organization. Some family businesses take the approach, "If it's good for one, we should do it for all." Some of these companies already have in place an employee-development program for nonfamily workers. That makes it easy to introduce intensive career-development activities for successors, since everyone is getting a similar chance. If development programs are new in your family business, you might view successor development as a test of the concept of employee development. If it works well for the successor generation, others might be allowed to take part as well.

An ideal solution is to focus the family's attention on the importance of management development. A good vehicle for this is a family meeting, as discussed in No. 2 of this series, *Family Meetings: How to Build A Stronger Family and A Stronger Business*. Once everyone understands the need to develop the potential of people working in the business and gets excited about the program, the next step is easy. If the family asks, "Where do we start?" incumbent business leaders can suggest, "We start with our kids. This is a gift to them."

Other family businesses take a more direct approach, stressing the importance of competent management. They may simply tell family members and employees, "These are the future leaders of the business, and they're going to get some special developmental experiences." While the message is blunt, stakeholders usually accept it. They may reason,

"If these kids are going to run the business, it's better that their capabilities be developed. If we're getting a new boss, we'd rather it be a good one."

Special Challenges to the Owner-Manager

Preparing someone else to take over your business can be a confounding challenge for many entrepreneurs. Let's take a look at some of the personal issues it raises.

What is the right role for me in all this? The first thing a business owner must do to develop successors is to organize and focus the process, make sure adequate resources are devoted to it, and set it in motion.

The second thing is to get out of the way.

Ideally, the parent should do a lot of listening and guiding the successor in the process of setting goals. Then, the parent should withdraw and let the successor "do his (or her) thing." Periodically, the two can meet again to talk about what is being accomplished and what might be done differently.

Resisting the impulse to control the successor by giving lots of advice and criticism or, worse yet, by trying to solve problems for him or her, is crucial. A successor doesn't need a parent looking on and handing out grades. A successor needs lots of rope.

But shouldn't I be deeply involved in teaching the successor? While successful business owners do many things well, they — like many parents — are often lousy teachers or coaches of their own mature children. **The art of teaching is the art of assisting discovery. It requires patience, and it demands activity by the student more than by the teacher. It requires letting go rather than taking charge, standing aside rather than wading in.**

The personality required to start or grow a business, on the other hand, works against effective teaching. Entrepreneurs are doers. They are impatient, take action, achieve goals and control outcomes. Frustrated by the task of teaching, one entrepreneur said, "I need to feel I'm always accomplishing something. I need to see the concrete results of my labors. How do you know you're contributing if all you're

> *The art of teaching is the art of assisting discovery. It requires letting go rather than taking charge, standing aside rather than wading in.*

doing is giving advice or responding to questions?" Successors see it differently. "Strong builders don't usually leave strong successors because the builders tend to dominate," according to a successor quoted by Patricia O'Toole in *Corporate Messiah* (Wm. Morrow, 1984). "They squelch creativity, they are often overassured and they brook no interference."

Parents also may feel so deeply responsible for their children's success that they blame themselves when their children fail. They may be too upbeat when evaluating their children, or else they are blind to the children's talents.

But if I'm not the right one to develop my successors, who could possibly be better prepared? Mentors, consultants, outside directors — any trusted and qualified outsider — is almost invariably a more effective teacher to the successor. Each can be guided by the personal-development plan that the business owner helps create and monitor. Periodic performance appraisals, particularly by nonfamily managers, are an excellent teaching tool as well. These outsiders experience none of the conflicts parents may face in preparing a successor.

Won't I be eager to prepare to hand over control to others? Probably not. In fact, the need to step back from controlling the successor's development often comes at a particularly difficult life stage for the business owner. **Late in the entrepreneur's career, self-doubt may grow, igniting a need to plunge into action and reassert one's value to the business.** A desire to "perfect" the business that has played such a huge role in the entrepreneur's life may overtake other impulses, propelling him or her into a whirlwind of managerial activity. This period may actually be the most difficult time of all for an entrepreneur to let someone else take even partial control over his or her "baby."

These internal struggles by the entrepreneur can be damaging if allowed to interfere with the successor's development. Implicitly, and sometimes explicitly through open criticism of the successor, the business owner is planting seeds of doubt about the future by trying to show everyone in the organization that he or she is indispensable. Even if the entrepreneur succeeds in rooting out the "imperfections" that trouble him or her, more harm than good has been done.

Won't my strong desire to help my kids succeed overshadow these problems? While many entrepreneurs consciously and surely want their children to succeed, they may unconsciously set them up to fail. A successor's inability to manage the business may satisfy the founder's

EXHIBIT 8 ■■■■■■■■■■■■■■■■■■■■■■■■■■■■■■■■■■■■■

Coaching Techniques for Parents

- When you see a problem, don't take steps to fix it. Wait for a private time and talk to the successor about it.

- Set regular meetings with your successor to discuss progress and problems.

- When the successor asks a question or shares a thought, respond only to the subject that has been raised. Don't dredge up other issues.

- Keep in mind that teachers — and great leaders — are known more by the success of their followers than by what they do themselves.

---

unconscious need to be proven indispensable or reassert his competence. "Unconscious" is the key word here. The father or mother may not be aware of needs that may be frustrated by the transfer of power. But they are powerful nonetheless, and doubly powerful when they are unconscious.

These conflicting desires, conscious and unconscious, can result in what may seem to others like erratic, contradictory behavior by the founder. He or she may give the successor lofty titles without pay and authority to match. The incumbent may undercut any initiatives that the successor takes, all the while promising that the corner office will soon be the successor's. This kind of behavior can poison parent-child relations, making the successor resentful, frustrated and restless, according to Harry Levinson, the noted organizational psychologist.

How about giving the successor a top job right at my elbow, such as "Assistant to the President," so he or she can learn by watching me? This kind of staff assignment for a successor is usually a mistake. The successor has no real job and no real responsibility. Just as bad, he or she reports to the parent, allowing little latitude to develop unique talents or complementary skills. The situation offers little opportunity to learn line responsibility or to earn authority.

But shouldn't my successor be as much like me as possible? **Many business owners think that to develop a successor, they must create someone just like themselves. This is not only impossible, but it**

EXHIBIT 9 ▐███████████████████████████████████

Suggestions for
Effective Successor Development

- Define your goals for the company, then let your successors know what they are.

- Recognize and acknowledge successors' accomplishments.

- Tolerate and even encourage differing points of view among your successors.

- Pay attention to the effect your actions have on your successors and, particularly, their spouses.

- Encourage learning as something that is not only acceptable but valued in your company.

- Make sure successors actually have responsible jobs that increase in responsibility as their abilities grow.

— Léon A. Danco, Ph.D.
The Center for Family Business
Cleveland, Ohio.

---

misses a major truth about the business world. Even if the business owner were to succeed in cloning himself or herself, the clone would likely be ill-equipped to deal with the future of the business. Things are simply changing too fast.

Why not avoid all the hassle by tossing the successor into a tough job to sink or swim? If you lived by your wits as an entrepreneur and graduated from the school of hard knocks, your inclination may be to thrust your offspring into the same crucible.

It may be wise to recall that the crucible is a lot deeper, wider and hotter than it was when you began. Now that you have built a business, much more is at risk than when you began with little or nothing. All the stakeholders in your company — shareholders, customers, employees, suppliers and your community — stand to lose if your business suffers from an ill-planned succession.

Few CEOs who have been tossed into the corner office in an abrupt and ill-planned manner would wish the experience on anyone they love or respect. Arthur Ochs Sulzberger Sr., chairman and CEO of the New York Times Co., said he was "shell-shocked" by being thrust into his job after the unexpected death of his brother-in-law. The company's flagship newspaper, *The New York Times*, was reeling from a prolonged strike at the time. After one day on the job, Mr. Sulzberger told his sister, "I made my first executive decision. I've decided not to throw up."

Mr. Sulzberger later helped plan a step-by-step career development path for his son, Arthur Jr., exposing him to all areas of the business and gradually increasing his responsibilities. When, after decades of preparation, Arthur Jr. took over as publisher of *The Times*, his father said, **"If you believe in the process of an orderly transition, then you have to 'transit.'** It gives me great fatherly pride to turn the publishership over to someone not only qualified, but a son."

Moreover, the "sink-or-swim" approach wastes the opportunity for the founder to pass on the benefit of experience that will be crucial in managing a maturing enterprise. And it fails to **capitalize on the enormous moral influence the older generation wields just by being present. While Mom and Dad are around, siblings are far less likely to squabble or to forget the ties that bind them. If contentious issues aren't resolved while the older generation is still present, all opportunity to find a peaceful solution may vanish and the issues may explode into damaging battles.**

Capitalize on the enormous moral influence the older generation wields just by being present.

Special Challenges
to the Successor

Joining the family business offers the rare opportunity to build one's own destiny on a foundation laid by previous generations.

Yet a successor's path isn't easy. The problems are unique. No one else knows what working for one's parent or gaining enormous business power at a young age are really like.

Most successors believe they have to work harder than anyone else. But they also often wonder where they stand. One third-generation president of a $180-million (sales) company had led the family business for a decade, but still wondered, "What does my Dad think of me as an executive?"

Consider these confidential comments from successors:

■ *"Being in the family business isn't as easy as many think ... They say it's lonely at the top, but it's also lonely being the son or daughter of the 'top.' Who can I talk to? Who can I trust?"*

■ *"Mom always wanted me to join the business. I didn't feel I had any other choice. But now, I wonder if I could even get hired anywhere else."*

■ *"No one taught me to be a president."*

■ *"I need a 55-year-old, wise, experienced shoulder to lean on."*

Some of the special challenges faced by successors have been described earlier, including revitalizing strategy and communicating, often for the first time, the vision and values guiding the family business. Let's take a look at some other issues.

Developing Self-Reliance. A rookie third baseman was warming up for his first game in the big leagues when a veteran shortstop overheard him mutter, "Boy, I hope no balls come to me."

After a pause, the veteran said, "Kid, when there's one out with the bases loaded, and you're up by one in the bottom of the ninth, that's when you should be hoping for a hot grounder. That's the only way you'll ever have a chance to win for your team.

"On the day you start hoping the ball comes to you — that's when you'll really be a pro."

Family business successors have a lot in common with the rookie.

Unproven and often untrusted by others in the business, yet thrust into positions of great power, they may shrink from responsibility. Yet at some point in the successor's personal development, there is no alternative to self-reliance. Chief executives have no one to show them the way.

As one family business successor turned 36, he began to wonder if he would ever take over the company. Though his father had assured him he would become president, guideposts on the path were lacking. "Dad says he wants to make sure I am ready before I take over," the successor says. "I keep asking him what he expects me to do to show that I am ready, but he will not be specific. He says he expects me to take initiative, to take responsibility, to provide direction. But while he says those things, he won't tell me how. What should I do?"

This successor needs to demonstrate his readiness to lead by carving out his own path to the top. This imperative arises for all successors at some point in their development. In some cases, the older generation may not have a successor-development plan nor even encourage anyone to prepare for leadership. In others, situations may arise that no development plan nor mentor can help with. At these times, the initiative must come from the successor.

Top companies build demands for self-reliance into successor development plans. At Anheuser-Busch Companies Inc., Chairman August Busch III insists that his son, August IV, show initiative to advance in management. The son's on-the-job training began at 15, driving a forklift at a wholesaler's warehouse, *Business Week* reported in a 1992 feature profile. Next, he shovelled wood chips out of beer tanks.

After college, August IV became the assistant to the company's top brewmaster. After a similar post in marketing, he headed a new-product launch and finally took over as product manager of the company's leading brand, Budweiser. His father calls him at all hours of the day and night to chew over marketing strategies. "There's not a day in the week when he doesn't ask me a question or give me a hard time about something," August IV says in the article.

The father's perspective: "There is no guarantee that August has a direct line of succession in this corporation." A colleague adds: "Does Aug have an advantage over a guy named Joe Corcoran? Yeah. But if he doesn't work his butt off, it won't happen."

Developing Your Own Identity. Successors' lives are filled with paradoxes:

Child or Troubleshooter? On one hand, successors are still under the tutelage of the older generation and subject to their elders' decisions. On

EXHIBIT 10

Some Suggestions for Learning Accountability

- Create your own source of income in high school or college.
- Design your own college goals in study, personal life and extracurricular activities.
- Work outside the family business for a while.
- Develop some job alternatives to working in the family business.
- Travel or enroll in personal-development programs.
- Ask to be paid market rates while working in the family business.
- Seek feedback whenever possible, though talking with peers, performance appraisals or incentive systems.

---

the other hand, to be an effective successor, they must figure out their parents' problems and — as diplomatically as possible — solve them for them. This dilemma is reflected by one successor's interpretation of his "job description":

"Dad's job is to do whatever he wants. My job is to do whatever he doesn't want to do. His performance is judged on how well he does in what he chooses to do. Mine is judged on how well I can guess what he won't get around to doing."

The Moving Target: The successor may feel frustrated in an entirely normal personal need to feel "in control" and "in charge." That feeling may continually elude you. You will never catch up with your parents in experience. They will always be 25 years or so ahead of you. You will have to learn to live with shooting at a moving target.

I Want My Own: Some successors also have to wrestle with their own entrepreneurial yearnings. Restlessness or impatience for greater responsibility can be a constant companion, especially when the successor is in his or her 30s and the incumbent, at 55, is years from retirement. Successors may feel deep in their hearts that they have the drive and ability to create something new — a business of their own. They wonder whether reinventing the family business will be satisfying enough.

EXHIBIT 11 ██████████████████████████████████

Dilemmas
Faced by Successors

Am I:

a child	or	a professional?
employees' peer	or	a privileged owner?
a subordinate	or	a boss?
lucky	or	worthy?
a clone	or	my own person?

Never Grown Up: Family relationships may continually interfere with the successor's efforts to establish a mature professional image. As one successor frustratedly put it, "I wish my aunt and father would just see me as any other employee. I'm embarrassed by some of the things they say to me in public!"

You Can't Win: The successor may never feel fairly credited with his or her accomplishments. **The founder's image as a hero, genius or saint may so permeate the business that the successor must struggle to make his or her own mark.** If successors succeed, they are seen by others as a "chip off the old block" who had all the breaks. If they fail, they are a discredit to the family.

In the early years of the successor's career, the only remedy may be an unshakable inner sense of identity — and a little humor. When Jack Nicklaus II was asked what it's like to be followed by a big crowd at a golf tournament because of his famous father, he said, "It's nice to have so many people watching. They can help me find my ball."

The Search Within. The best antidote to these feelings is a strong and secure self-knowledge. Each successor must examine his or her personal strengths and achieve some comfort with his or her own capabilities. He or she must **look for ways to develop an identity separate from the business and cultivate a healthy ego independent of family roles and relationships.**

A good start is to attain more formal education in an area in which the incumbent generation is weak. Mentors and work experience outside the

EXHIBIT 12 ████████████████████████████████

When Conflict Arises: Some Suggestions for the Successor

- Look for and reflect on any basic differences in values that may underlie your conflict with your parent.
- Join or form a support group of fellow successors to air and examine your problems.
- Draw upon your personal rationale for being in the family business.
- Seek advice confidentially from your parent's trusted peers or professional advisors.
- Engage in and draw on successes in industry, civic, community and religious activities to build self-esteem.
- Take opportunities to assume responsibility. Don't wait for someone to give it to you.

---

business can be invaluable in honing a strong sense of self. So can activities in religious, community and civic organizations.

Sometimes, other successors are the only ones who can suggest solutions to the problems a successor faces. Many successors find it helpful to join peer groups to share experiences and lend support. As indicated in the Resource List at the end of this booklet, The Executive Committee and the Young Presidents Organization are two such groups. Others form informal support groups of their own.

Inside the business, the successor must, of course, respect the incumbent generation's achievement. But he or she must also insist, in a mature and reasonable way, on the freedom and independence he or she needs to develop skills and responsibility. That can be acquired at the parent's elbow, in a separate unit, or away from the family business altogether. But it must be acquired.

Throughout this process, it is wise to avoid being too quick to label Mom or Dad "the problem." A far better approach is to try to identify their problems and solve them. This will go far in helping the successor gain a strong self-image, as well as earning acceptance and credibility within the organization. **The word "earn" is pivotal: the successor must demonstrate ability, people skills and stewardship in order to win the allegiance of employees and other stakeholders.**

Building the Business Skills of the Future. We asked attendees at a recent seminar for family business successors in their 20s and 30s to name the most crucial attributes for business leaders of the future. Given today's emphasis on professional management, one might have expected them to answer with a long list of business-school course titles such as marketing, finance, accounting or administration. Instead, they named responsibility, self-assurance, independence and accountability.

As these future business leaders knew, today's family business successors will be thrust into a crucible of constant change. No single formal discipline can fully prepare you for the changing and challenging business environment of the future. Instead, each successor must be responsible for his or her own continuing and lifelong development.

One of the most important skills for CEOs in such an environment is a capacity to learn as a lifelong endeavor. A business leader must be able continually to identify needed skills and knowledge and to acquire them. Adapting to change and cultivating a unique business culture are crucial. Just as important is learning how to develop one's own vision and philosophy for the business.

The successor also may have to alter the organization's leadership model from that of an individualistic 'loner" to that of a team leader. Coping with an increasingly diverse workforce and managing risk in an increasingly ambiguous world will be pivotal skills for the future as well.

Finding Personal Satisfaction in Leadership. "How can leadership ever be satisfying?" many successors wonder when confronted with accelerating change and uncertainty in the business environment. "How can it be fun to hold a job that is changing so much? Where is the personal satisfaction in all this?"

Many successors find today's business environment demands a management philosophy completely different from that of their parents. Some shift their personal goals, seeking their rewards in developing the people around them to the fullest and watching them grow. Others work out different personal rationales for coping with the stresses they face.

Successors need to be uncompromisingly honest with themselves about whether they want a top job in the family business. If they are taking the job to grab power or to satisfy a sense of obligation to perpetuate the family heritage, they are heading for trouble. **The successor must realize that he or she will have a fiduciary responsibility to shareholders in the business.** Shareholders, in effect, hire the successor to lead the family business. The successor in turn is obligated to recognize that relationship, build ties with shareholders, provide them with a compelling vision and strategy for the utilization of their assets, and meld them into a team.

EXHIBIT 13 ▄▄▄▄▄▄▄▄▄▄▄▄▄▄▄▄▄▄▄

Business Leadership
Skills of the Future

- How to learn
- Adapting to change
- Leading others
- Fostering teamwork
- Nurturing a healthy business culture
- Developing a philosophy of management

- Developing a vision for the future of the business
- Building a team
- Managing an increasingly diverse workforce
- Managing risk

If the successor does not want that kind of responsibility, he or she should make an effort to concentrate ownership in the hands of people who are in the business. Often, this is the best course of action. It can give managers the authority they need to do the job. An outside board can be extremely helpful in assessing the ownership structure of a family business and identifying needed changes.

Whatever the resolution, the successor needs to be both honest and clear in defining his or her commitment to the family's values and goals. When Arthur Ochs Sulzberger Jr. succeeded his father as publisher of *The New York Times*, he stated his own commitment: "I pledge my devotion to the precepts that make this paper great: the fairness and honesty of its journalism, the integrity of its journalistic practices, and the decency of its treatment of all individuals."

Part of the job of leading a family business is winning the commitment of all stakeholders in the business. You accomplish that by demonstrating competence and by letting stakeholders know that you have exciting plans for the future of the family business, a major collective resource. **If you succeed in that, you will emerge a new kind of hero.**

Summary

Preparing a new generation for family business leadership can be one of the toughest jobs a business owner ever faces. Yet it is critical to the continuity and revitalization of the business. The next generation of owner-managers will face the continuing challenge of revitalizing strategy in the face of accelerating change in the business environment. **This will require not only solid business and leadership skills, but a lifelong commitment to learning.**

Preparing successors to meet this challenge is a seven-stage process. During the first stage, childhood through age 25, values and attitudes toward the business are formed. This booklet focuses on the next three stages. First, the successor's entry into the family business usually occurs between 20 and 30 years of age. Then begin two more crucial stages: developing basic business skills, and cultivating the leadership skills that will be required of family business owners in the future. After that, selection and the transition to leadership occur. Finally, the cyclical process of successor development begins all over again with the next generation.

The successor should enter the family business in response to an offer to fill a job that is needed. The decision should be regarded as an important personal choice, and the successor should be allowed to choose free of coercion. A personal development plan incorporating specific goals, attitudes, skills and knowledge that need to be acquired should be prepared by the successor and a coach or mentor, with the oversight of incumbent leaders of the business. It should help the successor develop skills complementary to those of the business owner. It also should describe the process and timing for progress reviews. Trusted outsiders, including directors, industrial psychologists and consultants, can play uniquely helpful roles.

In the leadership development stages, the successor focuses more intensely beyond the present to the time when he or she will be responsible for the entire business. He or she needs to earn authority and credibility, either through innovation or step-by-step accomplishments. The successor also may begin to work more closely with other future family business leaders, developing teamwork and shared decisionmaking skills.

Successors play a central and often unique role in articulating the family business vision and philosophy, and in revitalizing strategy. Often, they are the first to put into words the significance of the family business's existence and survival. They often are the first to articulate a new strategic vision for the business to family members and other stakeholders.

The process of preparing successors for leadership places unique and heavy personal demands on members of both generations of family business leadership. Both business owners and successors need to be aware that they will face some intense challenges, and prepare to get the answers they may need to make the process go smoothly.

Resource List
for Successor Development

■ **American Management Association.** A wide range of one-day seminars on finance, marketing, management, sales and training for executives of companies with 20 to 250 employees, as well as a monthly publication, Small Business Reports. Contact: Marlene Sholod, Director, Programs for Growing Companies, American Management Association, 135 W. 50th St., New York, NY 10020-1201. (212) 586-8100.

■ **Babson College.** Undergraduate and graduate courses in entrepreneurship and family business management, as well as a three-day residential program for owner-managers and other executives in small and growing businesses. Contact: Irene McCarthy, Administrative Director, The Center for Entrepreneurial Studies, Babson College, Babson Park, MA 02157-0310. (617) 239-4549.

■ **Baylor University.** Semi-annual family business conferences, a quarterly newsletter and weekend retreats on specific family business issues. Contact: Nancy Bowman-Upton, Director, or Fadene Shirley, Program Coordinator, Center for Family Business Studies, Baylor University, P.O. Box 98011, Waco, TX 76798. (817) 755-2265.

■ **Canadian Association of Family Enterprise.** Sponsors forums, workshops, social events and Personal Advisory Groups of 10 to 12 executives from non-competing companies to meet and share experiences and ideas. Contact: CAFE National, 615 Yonge St., 5th Floor, Toronto, Ontario M4Y 2T4. (416) 966-0661.

■ **Center for Creative Leadership.** A wide range of training programs, seminars and workshops at four locations, including leadership and management development, effecting change, creativity, organizational skills, working with others and promoting teamwork. Contact: Client Relations, Center for Creative Leadership, 5000 Laurinda Drive, P.O. Box 26300, Greensboro, NC 27438-6300. (919) 545-2810.

■ **Dale Carnegie & Associates Inc.** Courses on self-motivation, sales, customer relations, employee development, management, executive image and professional development. Contact: Dale Carnegie & Associates Inc., 1475 Franklin Ave., Garden City, NY 11530-1613. (516) 248-5100.

■ **The Executive Committee.** An invitation-only association of business owners, presidents and CEOs of companies ranging from $2 million to $1 billion in sales who meet to discuss business problems, exchange ideas, hear speakers and suggest solutions to each other's problems. Contact: Membership Coordinator, The Executive Committee, 3737 Camino del Rio South, Suite 206, San Diego, CA 92108. (800) 274-2367.

■ *The Family Business Advisor.* A monthly newsletter on successful business management, family relations and asset protection. Contact: The Family Business Advisor, P.O. Box 4356, Marietta, GA 30061-4356. (800) 551-0633.

■ **Harvard University.** Offers owner-managers of companies with $3 million to $100 million sales a series of management courses, including case studies, in three three-week units, usually completed in three consecutive years. Contact: Administrative Director, Owner/President Management Program, Soldiers Field — Glass Hall, Harvard Business School, Boston, MA 02163. (617) 495-6450.

■ **Kennesaw State College Family Enterprise Center.** Its Family Business Academy is a periodic, week-long program on family business management devoted specifically to helping successors become successful leaders. Its Family Business Forum is a membership group for family firms offering quarterly seminars, a newsletter and other services. Contact: Alyssa Barnes, Director, Management Development Center, Division of Continuing Education, Kennesaw State College, P.O. Box 444, Marietta, GA 30061. (404) 423-6559.

■ **Loyola University Chicago.** Meetings and small group forums especially for successors, among other programs for the entire family. A membership organization for family-owned Chicago-region firms with at least 200 employees. Contact: Drew Mendoza, Family Business Center, Loyola University Chicago, P.O. Box 257608, Chicago, IL 60625-7608. (312) 604-5005.

■ **Oregon State University.** Workshops, retreats and educational materials on all aspects of family business management. Contact: Patricia Frishkoff or Bonnie Brown, Co-Directors, Family Business Program, College of Business, Oregon State University, Bexell Hall 201, Corvallis, OR 97331-2603. (503) 737-3326.

■ **Outward Bound.** Personal and professional development through challenging adventure-based programs that cultivate self-respect, compassion for others and concern for the environment. Custom-designed management training programs available. Contact: Peg Howell, Outward Bound USA, 1536 Woodcrest Drive, Reston, VA 22094. (703) 787-7935 or (800) 779-7935.

■ **Owner-Managed Business Institute.** Offers educational programs in family business and general management, as well as a quarterly newsletter and consulting services. Contact: John Rinaldi, Owner-Managed Business Institute, 226 E. De La Guerra St., Santa Barbara, CA 93101. (800) 843-6624.

■ **Stanford University.** Offers the Executive Program for Smaller Companies, a two-week management program for senior executives who run small-to-medium-sized businesses with 50 to 1000 employees. Contact: Ms. Alyce Adams, Office of Executive Education, Graduate School of Business, Stanford University, Stanford, CA 94305-5015. (415) 723-9356.

■ **Toastmasters International.** Programs to help participants overcome the fear of public speaking by giving impromptu speeches to small groups. Training materials and other support provided. Contact: Marketing Manager, Toastmasters International, P.O. Box 9052, Mission Viejo, CA 92690. (714) 858-8255.

■ **University of Southern California.** Graduate and undergraduate courses in entrepreneurship, including entrepreneurial management, writing a business plan and understanding the business. Contact: James E. Porter, The Entrepreneurship Program, University of Southern California, Bridge Hall, Room 6, Los Angeles, CA 90089-1421. (213) 740-0643.

■ **University of Pennsylvania.** Seminars in executive education, as well as the Wharton Family Business Network program, which draws family business owners and managers for two-day management sessions four times a year. Contact: Carol Vassian, Director, Sol C. Snider Entrepreneurial Center, The Wharton School, University of Pennsylvania, 426 Vance Hall, 3733 Spruce St., Philadelphia, PA 19104. (215) 898-4470.

■ **Yale University.** Offers programs in leadership, decisionmaking, conflict resolution, interpersonal communications, and understanding management issues in the context of a global economy. Contact: Program Coordinator, Executive Education Office, Yale School of Organization and Management, Box 1A, New Haven, CT 06520-7368. (203) 432-6038.

■ **Young Presidents Organization.** Groups of company presidents meet to share ideas and information. New members must be under 44 years of age and must have become president of their businesses before the age of 40. Members "graduate" at the age of 50. Contact: General Offices, Young Presidents Organization, 451 S. Decker Drive, Irving, TX 75062. (214) 541-1808.

■ **Other Programs for Family Businesses:**
  • Bryant College Institute for Family Enterprise. Smithfield, RI 02917. (401) 232-6477.
  • Center for Family Business. Cleveland, OH 24268. (216) 442-0800.
  • Goshen College Family Business Program. Goshen, IN 46526. (219) 535-7451.
  • Memphis State University Mid-South Family Business Forum. Memphis, TN 38152. (901) 678-2432.
  • Northeastern University Center for Family Business. Dedham, MA 02026. (617) 320-8019.
  • Susquehanna University Family Business Center. Selinsgrove, PA 17870. (717) 374-0101.
  • University of Cincinnati Goering Center for Family/Private Business. Cincinnati, OH 45221. (513) 556-7180.
  • University of San Diego Family Business Institute. San Diego, CA 92110. (619) 260-4644.

Index

The Authors

Craig E. Aronoff and John L. Ward have long been recognized as leaders in the family business field. Founding principals of the **Family Business Consulting Group**, they work with hundreds of family businesses around the world. Recipients of the Family Firm Institute's Beckhard Award for outstanding contributions to family business practice, they have spoken to family business audiences on every continent. Their books include *Family Business Sourcebook* II and the three-volume series, *The Future of Private Enterprise.*

Craig E. Aronoff, Ph.D., holds the Dinos Eminent Scholar Chair of Private Enterprise and is professor of management at Kennesaw State University (Atlanta). He founded and directs the university's Family Enterprise Center. The center focuses on education and research for family businesses, and its programs have been emulated by more than 100 universities worldwide. In addition to his undergraduate degree from Northwestern University and Masters from the University of Pennsylvania, he holds a Ph.D. in organizational communication from the University of Texas.

John L. Ward, Ph.D., is Clinical Professor of Family Enterprises at Northwestern University's Kellogg Graduate School of Management. He is a regular visiting lecturer at two European business schools. He has also previously been associate dean of Loyola University Chicago's Graduate School of Business, and a senior associate with Strategic Planning Institute (PIMS Program) in Cambridge, Massachusetts. A graduate of Northwestern University (B.A) and Stanford Graduate School of Business (M.B.A. and Ph.D.), his *Keeping the Family Business Healthy* and *Creating Effective Boards for Private Enterprises* are leading books in the family business field.

The best information resources for business-owning families and their advisors

The Family Business Leadership Series
Concise guides dealing with the most pressing challenges and significant opportunities confronting family businesses.

Comprehensive — Readable — Thoroughly Practical
- *Family Business Succession: The Final Test of Greatness*
- *Family Meetings: How to Build a Stronger Family and a Stronger Business*
- *Another Kind of Hero: Preparing Successors for Leadership*
- *How Families Work Together*
- *Family Business Compensation*
- *How to Choose & Use Advisors: Getting the Best Professional Family Business Advice*
- *Financing Transitions: Managing Capital and Liquidity in the Family Business*
- *Family Business Governance: Maximizing Family and Business Potential*
- *Preparing Your Family Business for Strategic Change*
- *Making Sibling Teams Work: The Next Generation*
- *Developing Family Business Policies: Your Guide to the Future*
- *Family Business Values: How to Assure a Legacy of Continuity and Success*
- *More Than Family: Non-Family Executives in the Family Business*
- *Make Change Your Family Business Tradition*
- New guides on critical issues published every six to twelve months

The Family Business ADVISOR Monthly Newsletter

Family Business Sourcebook II
Edited by Drs. Aronoff and Ward with Dr. Joseph H. Astrachan, *Family Business Sourcebook II* contains the best thoughts, advice, experience and insights on the subject of family business. Virtually all of the best-known experts in the field are represented.

Now Available:
John Ward's Groundbreaking Family Business Classics
- *Keeping The Family Business Healthy*
- *Creating Effective Boards For Private Enterprises*

For more information:
Family Enterprise Publishers, P.O. Box 4356, Marietta, GA 30061
Tel: 800-551-0633 or 770-425-6673